Fiddledeedee

fiddledeedee

Shelby Stephenson

Press 53
Winston-Salem

Press 53, LLC
PO Box 30314
Winston-Salem, NC 27130

First Edition

Copyright © 2014 by Shelby Stephenson

Fiddledeedee was first published by
The Bunny and the Crocodile Press, Washington, D.C.,
© 2001 by Shelby Stephenson

All rights reserved, including the right of reproduction in whole or in part in any form except in the case of brief quotations embodied in critical articles or reviews. For permission, contact author at editor@Press53.com, or at the address above.

Cover design by Kevin Morgan Watson

Cover art, "Fiddledeedee,"
Copyright © 2014 by Hayden Tedder,
used by permission of the artist.

Author photo by Jeff Davis

Cover artist photo by Keith Sherard

Printed on acid-free paper
ISBN 978-1-941209-17-2

to Fred Chappell

Acknowledgments

Some parts of *Fiddledeedee* have appeared, sometimes in different form, in the following publications:

Albatross
Ampersand
The Arts Journal
Cairn
Cardinal: A Contemporary Anthology
A Carolina Literary Companion
The Chattahoochee Review
Gambit
Half Tones to Jubilee
Iron Mountain Press (Broadside)
Loblolly
The MacGuffin
The Manhattan Review
El Nahuatzen
New Virginia Review (Anthology)
Oyster Boy Review
Poet & Critic
Poetry Northwest
Poetry Under the Stars (Anthology)
The Review
St. Andrews Review
Sandpaper Magazine
256 Shades of Grey
The Signal
The Texas Review
The Thomas Wolfe Review
Tsiskari (The Dawn) [The Republic of Georgia]
Willow Springs
The Worcester Review
Z Miscellaneous

Some of *Fiddledeedee* appeared in a chapbook called *Carolina Shout!* winner in 1985 of a statewide chapbook competition sponsored by The Playwright's Fund of North Carolina and the North Carolina Arts Council.

Special thanks to Grace Cavalieri and The Bunny and the Crocodile Press/Forest Woods Media Productions, Inc. for publishing a limited edition of *Fiddledeedee* in 2001. And to Cynthia Comitz, *In Support, Inc.* for her work in preparation of that original manuscript and to George Klear who printed it at *Printing Press, Inc.*

*The flowers appear on the earth,
the time of singing has come,
and the voice of the turtledove
is heard in our land.*

—The Song of Solomon

*Fiddledeedee, Fiddledeedee,
The fly has married the bumblebee.*

—Mother Goose Nursery Rhyme

fiddledeedee

prologue

SAYING I NEED AN IMAGE TO MAKE THE WORLD
I went back home and held my eyes on the hill
and it said You need a word deeper than *I*

so I took the old fencerails the lizards ran
and my family's tongue came out of the Mouth
of Buzzard's Branch, the sound of that one story,

everywhere, in the marshes, in the fields
and lowgrounds, and I said Where is the word
that holds All I am trying to say?—

and the cows lowed through their cuds over
and over *it is nothing but a song*—the long journey home:
Slow Man Barbour rode his Cushman

pooter-scooter and parked it when we played
cow-pasture ball: I used to run in from the hayfield
to see what Ralph Kiner had done that day:

he was *my* man to break the Babe's homerun
mark, a chance to have somebody stand up
to bat for me: can I make a motion

for home, motion, the third-base coach might say
is slow, out of time, the squeak and sound of
footsteps—my wife coming home, coming to a place

we call *home*? The shifting winds catch her voice
full in her breasts; dark-throated locusts
dusk their beasts of sounds—home in the spine

which sitteth uneasily, the body
sensual still, all those mockingbirds
riffling feathers at the first suggested intrusion,

the low footage, getting a toe-hold *this place
will be yours someday* and here we are, the workers
mostly gone, the Bee Martin

out on the marker at the end of the drain,
catching insects come home to rest: I was
born in that house in the hedge, the dogyard

outback, the mulestables, chickens running
free, the hogpen homey with grunts and
tail-twitches—that's it, the tall pile of wood

Percy Bolling cut for the stove in the kitchen,
the Home Comfort Range, that's it, home,
the humming presence of overriding lips

the hymns my mother would sing while stirring
the soup: coming home is a hard row to hoe,
middle to bust, blossom to top, barn to fill,

road to pave, push to shove: the tractor's
ready for the pasture, the bush-hog levels the field:
the lay is home, the lying down to sleep,

counting sheep, roughshod hooves grazing the top
rail of the fence *hum on* Percy would say,
Butler and Tony trailing the possum

hum on home, you good dogs you (of all those
thirty-five hounds we never had a dog
named Blue): the cotton's tied up in burlap

sheets waiting to be weighed: my mother picked
385 pounds in one day!
How, I said, could you do that and she said

Well, we'd be in the field early when the dew
was on the bolls and the cotton weighed more:
in a flash Marshall Brown's hat goes up the

chute at the old Ogburn Gin. "Uhhhh," he said,
his head uncapped, crown gone, bare: he was embarrassed:
What is a man without his hat—I can't

go home, Eloise won't know me: a fury
of heat August spreads out like some massive
transformer: an occasional leaf falls

and I am leaving to seek new fortunes
in the fortuitous faddle with feeling
fiddling sweet strains seeking you seeking me,

looking back, darling, to see if you are
looking back to see, calling my name,
the old perceptions laid low, gone over the years

to the shallows, the depth-finders, all the way
to the homing ruin of runs rampart
in the boxscores, the old families dying out,

pushing up roots: come quietly as a visitor
and look for me under your footfalls:
my mother's father hanged himself by a

cow-rope jumping off the hogshed, she only
six, waiting for the schoolbus, lingering
and scuffling the sand in the path there

the way little children do, and her brother,
running to the parlor, the hogs disarrayed,
the slops and corn spilled under the man's dangling

feet, what he must have seen was everything—
home, county, school, country, the pledge of allegiance,
his dinner-bucket—whatever held

him to the starched world his mother made went
haywire and home became a desperate
survival for the mother and seven

children: we carry the graveyards and the
corridors of the gone so long: stones in
cedar-bemused cemeteries throughout

the country, my country of thee, ours,
the hour departing ever: see the corners
of the old house fall away, windows

open to the corn and hay, crumpled debris,
1952, sweet harsh wind coming
around the corner of the kitchen, the house

itself a solitude in the mist—what
tin so rusty and quiet: smokescreen, please,
peas porridge, ridges hot, please, papa, ridge

the rows, *row row* "plashless," she said—Mary's
tuffet, the fat and the lean Sprats, the cat
in the boat, the winking moon writing

my life away in the woozy weight of going
home *home home sweet home there's no place* home is
a valley around a bend, a round of

sunrises: how we got by on what we
had until the father, gone, mother, too,
gone from this world, an empty house I have

no image for, not knowing if coming
back would be a place at home, homeplace, plate,
stance, mark—how do I get home—don't move an

inch: go straight and turn, turning in the wide
net the blackbirds knot in the sky over
the roiling water of hogkills, the vat

bubbling a hot song of meat and death,
the least rust on the tin, iridescent,
the sun cutting the outbuildings into lengths,

shadows dancing on the ground *eerie there
everywhere* sitting on the wrap-around
porch, a tune humming, the farmer singing

behind the plow and cursing the way home,
the years, thirty so far with her: hum, ham,
hock *hock on Sounder gittem boy hemem up*

hot, heat, grave, gravy, hearth, hope, fire, blue and
green in conversation's ire—home, the place
where the bird went out of his mind diving

for the bug under the dusk-to-dawn light,
nights to keep, the bed a quilt of soft pressure,
the lovers beside themselves, the mouse scurrying:

doom, a dam to thought, a thought too dim to light
a credence to precedence *my mama
was hanging out clothes when I got home my

mama was on her toes stretching to hang
out clothes the clothesline sagged with Mama
on her toes hanging out clothes* look at the

cushiony thighs of lawn, leg of dirt-green,
a closure after the hurricane's surge,
trees down everywhere: lead me on and let

me stand: take chances, loose and gangly, some
water from the branch to bubble at the
spring, the john flushed with a flip of the bucket,

the timely tension, the drag of being
unwashed and uncouth, unkempt, unfed, deals
undone and beds unmade: we distance

each to each what there is left: the tone of
things to come is the coming tone, time, rhyme
rending the simple treasure of a story

forgot, ever the one leaf never to
stem: veins swell and contract, September peas
harden in the pods: walk out to the awe-sided

air and breathe, dig deeply for the earth's
concealment, anneal the healing flow,
the underground run of water out

to the ditch and down the hill: run the fox:
hear the music as the dogs chase the red
to the limit, tense muscles: the mules bear

down to pull the timber out of the swamp,
their hooves sucking back home's spatial
whirligig, sanctuary of the real, the

reeling calm: there is a plan here, of course,
some vivid virtue knowledge powers and
wills without imposition, the washpot

ready with boiling water, hogfat, a
lardy, caky pot full of soap as certain
as the butcher-knife slices she cut, my

body feeling October's frosted, fragile
spider-webs in the viburnum after surgery
strong and tight, recovery—this place

so changing: the hydrangea at the backstoop
droops for me: time to shuffle out of the study,
padding evenly in my slippers: once

there was mule-time, skinny lines going
with the reins, the green-scented, blinking
farts when Gray would spraddle her legs: debris

scatters little rivers running away:
the creek rocks the Roach Branch where my father
lay on his stomach to drink, his hat

pillowed under his chest—the leaves leaving
the stream's mouth to another leggy spill.

fiddledeedee

OUT OF AN INCREMENTAL MEMORY
I sing the outgoing redness of childhood
never forming in one visible image,

yet definite as the hayfield offering
its ritual, real in an unimaginary
way, for getting up hay never interested

me, the dust in my lungs, my sweaty shirt
itching: I entered the world itching,
confused as I still am, figuring in

the lower swamp a deeper meaning
with my companions, my probings lost in the taunts
I'd let bounce like sticks thrown on brick:

*hey red on the head like the dick under
a dog's belly, runt, freckles, crosseyes, four eyes,
smoke, chub,* and as I grew I said yes and yes again

until all the bullies in me at Cleveland School
melted in a vat with hogs
roiling in chains on killing day, a ritual

discovering the self I can never touch,
that dark evil light that glows in eggs mornings
when the sun is right and the chicken is pipping:

the egg hatched and the chicken's bones raised
up into one dazzling world
from the hopping flea wanting a place to stop

to the remaining apple blossoms
scattering like crumbs from God's table:
I was born June 14, 1938

Flag day, in the sign of the Gemini,
on the Wheel of Changing Change, in a pure
accident, one identity coming out of the other

as a river of youth runs in a river of
death, Nature created out of the self's mask,
one protean being turning me into a

giant when I'd read about Jack and his cow,
and into a man when I'd see the hulk
of a man under the coat, in the contest between the sun

and the wind, the sun winning, and I'd feel the
helpless helper in myself integrated in the perfect motion,
its tendencies never to be finished in and out of itself:

a June child embodies the opposites,
confounding us always to see
the grave and humorous on the threshold of

art about to form out of the counterpoise,
to leave a deposit with earning power:
look hard in the glory of your means:

I was gotten my father said
from "pulling out not soon enough"
and that was enough to get me started:

said my ears were so big he put me
on the top doorstep to see if I would
fly the long swallow up the shadow-grown

loft of my crib, growing among blackbirds
(four and twenty), crows cawing through
the duck-walking years, the burrowing

owl's whooooo my ears knew the sound
in the fencerow *that lonesome whippoorwill
he sounds too blue to fly* while the front stoop

my father set me on fell down every time
someone placed a foot on the bottom step,
unnailed like everything else, the hump-throated

fishhawk loping on to whatever ruffed grouse
could work peripheries:
the mourning doves settle their wings like shields,

their sight on me: fly on, fly on–you nighthawks,
orioles, ospreys–oh the diving
die-does of grebes and the died-apples

(my father called them) of the apple orchard
(they would flop down as if broken-winged
and swing up and out through the trees, a rotting

apple in their beaks): fly on
purple martin for the insects over the house
Grandpa William made for you

and set high on a pole over the
garden of black earth at the Old Place,
my red-bellied woodpecker-self in the fall sun, haying,

my skin blistering, rose-breasted,
road-running, rough-winged, redheaded,
red-throated, laughing at the common snipe

I am, the times I have been left holding the bag,
times I have seen the wide net I pitched go
up in a lark of knots, drunk in

a flutter of wings, my sparse hair
tickling like new bird stubble: sparrows fly round
my head twelve out of twenty-four through one ear

and out the other and they warble as they fly:
blue coots whistle, bleat, and groan
O if warble could find the hermited

black-throated commonwealth of noise
what dominion of ugly happy tyranny would befall
those birds pitching on the top doorstep:

there is no way around the roots in the yard,
a waterboy holding the bucket for his father
to drink, the mules bent over the grass,

the muzzles on a nail under the shelter:
I've been on many a mule in my time:
I'd sit behind the gummed collar, on the hot,

sweaty backband, the traces jingling and
my empty pockets stuck together:
Black and Gray never had brass balls crowning

the hames, as some mules did, but I held on
to what was there: John said that's good enough:
you must ride for the air between your ass

and the withers, otherwise the world will beat
you to death: this is life, and there is no
theory for it: the night was clear as the stars

in my reach from the middle room: we took baths
every Saturday night in a wooden washtub
set in the center of the pantry where

the Warm Morning Range presided, the eyes
one-pronged, waiting for my mother to poke
the handle in the socket and put more wood

on the fire, the pots and pans sizzling:
one night I stayed with Uncle Rubin:
he'd sit by the woodstove, tilt his chair

back against the pantry door, dip snuff
and read the Bible: he looked far away:
they put us to bed in the different smells:

I sat up like a young bird about to be left
alone to fall or fly: I did neither,
maybe a sideways glance to say I am

lost on this featherbed, fading like a rain
drop on ink, a watermelon (July ham,
I heard Merle Travis say once), coolness

in a foot tub, a can of cut bait forgotten
in the sun: Jesus comes when the time is right,
the vision wide without snares, the corn tall

beyond the outhouses, stacked fodder, the preachers
so many for me, for my father, his Bibles
on the chifforobe, the hymns I do not

remember they are so much a part of me—
sacred songs with *kneel* in every line almost:
the experience flies me forward into a past

I cannot let go: I cannot see heaven,
I could not, no matter how hard Preacher Mills
sawed the air with his hands: I sat my guilty self

where no preacher could help but set me free
in my sweet glowings under the cowshed
overhang when I was a boy: it would

be drizzling and I would get goosepimples,
my feelings were so strong: I'd dream and the
reverie would come out of itself

as the corn in the crib settled into
a workchant: hit the corn on the stalk
with a gloved hand, walk, and hit the next ear

with another, grunt and hear the help
together in the field songs: *Mary weeped
and Martha moaned, Sally got choked*

with a chicken bone up and back, back and up,
around, the rows heaped with corn, heaps of corn:
the fields wither in the heat: the wheelbarrow

is rusty against the shed, the chimney
fallen through the pack house: September
we'd bundle tobacco there and listen

to WCKY, Cincinnati:
hello, friends and neighbors in radioland,
Lonnie Glosson and Wayne Raney here,

playing some of your old-time country music:
before our first number, let me tell you
how you can get a genuwine Lord's Last Supper

table cloth picturing all the disciples,
including Judas: the sun looks for a place
to settle in the pine tree in the yard,

hanging there over the pine needles, the light
as lost as the two truck drivers who came
up from Savannah looking for Pride & Trimble:

I want to be ready, Lord, to walk in
Jerusalem just like John, be the least
one in: late summer is a long way back

in the vegetation of the earth: the wheels
in the fields are cuspidors spilling snuff
from all the courthouses in the South, the heat

beyond the beached high sand a welcome relief
from the gravel parking lots of the spirit
which is the body—one whole portion,

as Poe said: so I said to myself, get
down into the last place imaginable
and leave yourself in the open where

the raindrops preceding a storm will touch
you in an onrush of inspiration
from the racks of clouds black overhead:

how do the birds fare in this kind of weather?
When the storm comes they are gone and when our storm
comes we are gone, so many table crumbs

brushed among the swinging vines, the ground littered
with hulls, and the swinging was better than wine
as we'd wander down the path, popping the

fecund grapes in our mouths, the lower primings
of tobacco curing in the barns, a smell
of harvest exaggerating the world

lost from the center, smoke everywhere,
rising out of the source, a mere longing
in our nostrils, a slight breeze keeping manhood

back a little longer: truth stayed low
like a log while we quibbled over returns
and waited for the night, realizing

the obstacle at the core, the filled heart,
shattering at times beyond the soul's and
body's capacity to come round again:

you'd come with guano sacks the fertilizer
came in, the people said, with numbers on them:
3-9-6, 10-10-10, and you'd dip the burlap

(you always washed sacks at the Rock Hole) and
somehow a vision of John lowering
Jesus would appear next to the rock, a hole

of water lowering itself, a source of life:
what artistry seeps through the world we have
little to do with except to set ourselves

out in whatever time there is: we work
and wait for the night needing a place to
let go until the circle closes: I'd

turn over in the morning and someone
else had died, it seems; I had gone up to
see Uncle Shorty: a canary-yellow

Ford Crestliner was parked in the weeds:
it looked like a ship in a chicken yard:
Uncle Shorty was lying there, his face

the Stephenson oval, black hair, nose prominent
as the handle-end of a hammer, polished:
the new linoleum odor, the cut flowers,

the car's yellow I cannot escape: I
pictured Shorty under the clay roots in
Middle Creek, before he had his stroke, kicking

his feet out like a terrapin, shooting off here
and there, grinning when he'd come up for air:
I was under the walnut tree when the announcement

came that Hank Williams was dead: I was charmed
to hear that one who sang on the radio
could die: "I'm So Lonesome I Could Cry,"

"The Lovesick Blues," "Cold, Cold Heart," "I Can't Help It,"
"Rambling Man," "I Saw the Light," "I'll Never
Get Out of this World Alive": let's have a reunion

here, before the strokes and aches get too
heavy to bear, before the goodbyes and
perilous highs: what charity! Emily,

what are you up to, your hands gathering
fire beyond the late Amherst edge drawing
away tomorrow: up, Emerson, time to go:

whoa, goat, the hot is on again, though I
cannot see the path: if a bend would come
I could walk around and stop under the willow

and watch where the tips have brushed the sand:
I look up at the sky and want the rain
to fall so the corn may unroll, the tobacco

lift its leaves, and the potato vines raise
their red runners like dog hairs when another
enters the territory and stops, looks around

as if to say This is where I come in,
buddy, you'll have to move on, vamoosey:
the syllables go bouncy, the song wobbles

to tumble like someone's voice saying Wait
for me to come around to myself: a bird
ruffles its feathers on a rain bough, a dog

shimmies its body fast to groom after sleep:
the waking world catches on electric
wire strung around the pasture like a necklace,

a cradle and a burying ground, a chimney
standing in the rubble, a world stopped at one end,
breath at the other: the growing is within,

until there is nothing left to do
but let nature include what has not spoiled
all our born days, ourselves, untainted meat:

I remember the saltbox in the right-hand
corner of the corncrib, the hams, shoulders,
sides, hocks, jowls, heads, tails, ears, feet, backbones, maws,

all white in the salt all over: if we
killed hogs at the wrong time we risked the meat
going bad: sometimes skipper flies would bore

into the shoulders and my mother would take
the handsaw and cut out the tainted part,
but it never tasted right after that:

it was tainted as the world is, though I
quest for love, for my whole self to open
without hurt or prejudice, certain that

some faithful soul will straighten my longings:
a bird in the mouth is a misfit:
Lester Coats stands at a dirt crossroads, hollering,

"That's Jay Boy, boys, yonder's Jay Boy,"
and the fox crosses: Merton Byrd hollers,
the fox is caught, my father blows the horn:

looking for the sweat to lift, I see
the bushes spreading, the tick sucking the dog:
run, Mac, run: the morning violets climb

the trellis, the inseparable days
I set sail with, throwing my crutch away
until there is a hand, unwithered, to help

Uncle Shorty along, wait for his year
to make a slogan and bust out beyond
the buzzards circling the field: the repeating

shade shows widening unrest: see the dust
on the Bible: go for the long ride in
the scattering trust: there is time for the

considerable joy the body craves,
the points of departure we know will give us
a chance in the morning: take it: inhabit

the earth in the measured intention of the heart:
the melting time is now: somewhere the sunlight
hits the morning mirror with configurations

as big as the soul: my mother would hold
me up to the heater and wrap my body
in a blanket and lead me to the middle room

and I fell asleep knowing the house cared:
geese strutted the air and I lilted through
the night, Ophelia-eyed, mooning the morn,

the brisk brown eastward surprises in the
trees changing coats, moving their tongues slightly
in the breeziness up and around the

soft edges of the world crumpled like a
puppet's nose: What can we do but sing?
I will wear red more and carry my songs

in the minstrel's way: the leap conquers space:
we can forgive ourselves, seek mercy
from suffering races unrun, while bands

wait to strike up the music until the self
nestles in its bed without curse or need
for saving grace, the human predicament fed,

the whole rush out from life's table a chance
to prepare ourselves: the way to open
the day is to believe you'll get through,

the serious quest for hope heaped up on
the thin lines of our walks down familiar paths,
the best routine after all the years of waiting,

when the self is nobody, the feeling
gone within the broad dumb stage of creation,
the furrow empty of the seed and the

grave an empty likeness of the soul:
watch the duplication appear in a
symmetrical pattern when the sun unrolls

on the hedges: colors variously shape:
rumblings and stirrings, strings of energy
gather around me, the hillside sloping

up and down my body: the world's so finely
balanced a beetle could push it along:
let go the usual unusual

before our narrower selves settle for
something less than divine's whole measure:
the house will roll with instinct from the second

story when we are gone and the mice
multiply in pink in every cranny
clear to the pond, bass jumping out of the lilies

when the basset barks and my son says Thought
you wanted to fish, throwing a Mister
Twister toward the cattails where the kittens

shake their scrawny hides: yes, said the startled air
the redwing leaves, yes, said the rubber decoy
bouncing on a rope anchored to the pond's bottom,

no said the dogfly bit my cheek so red
the freckles flushed, maybe, the sun soaked
my shirt to gnaw my skin and the wind rolled

my hair through answers bright and thin:
the basset scratched its right ear for mites
and sadly put an image without deception

over my eyes and I could see the fish's path,
the water so ripply there, waves erasing
and replacing waves, the water so ripply

I could see the whining and the whispering
of the reel: the spiritual sight depends
in this world on the holy sight of

clairvoyance which is linked to the imagination
and its various parts, such as wings, body,
the fantastic beings, so that when the

down-and-outer stares into his hand and says
Why me, Lord, he sees his palm a mirror
of himself holding his other, protecting

his dumpled life, the end and beginning
coming together in his furrows, the
clods falling against his brogans, the hope

contemporary yet prehistoric
as the first ground broken: I'd put on the
yearly shoes and say Look at me now:

my old self says do not be sentimental:
you are going through the center where the
boy and the man meet, and they shall go

together here, doubling for no special
effect except to sense the heart always
forming the focal point: the Egyptians

left the heart in the mummy and from the
periphery of the unmoved presence
lying there, truth would explain everything,

the sun being the heart, the place to enter
for meditation and oneness, depths swelling
in the well attached to the high plank porch

of our shanty, well of muddy rope and
tickle: time the bucket rim first, bottom
back on the curb and in one form fill the

waiting pail with cool, clear water, the deep
weeping rain falling lowest under the
tin roof where Jim, the chicken-eating mule,

stops to drink: he trots out of the muck to
dry land, where falls keep tearing down the hillside:
fixed your roof? Naw, it don't need fixing now

*cause it ain't raining and when it's raining
I caint!* The native sun is pouring
Sundays and the mules are sweaty, the

tractors dusty, the federal pens pentup
with prisoners who want to write their
Penrod Was Here beyond the lowest

common denominator: at the blackboard
in the third grade, Mrs. Mina J. Higgins
said divide something by something and

I could not and she slapped me: she didn't know
how dumb I was and cold for love: birth and
death have no opinion: love is hate,

evil is good, martyrdom is ecstasy,
just as outer is inner and below
without above is not a proper home;

hum and silence is at hand, the supreme
diction, for the parody and the serious
are one, Finch's Mash echoed through the stench

which hangs near the Simmon Tree Hole, my sweet
water of channelcats, eels, horsefish,
whistledicks, bluegills, bass, horneyheads, and

bowfins, my old shoes left off too long, glad
to find the one right foot, root the self in
oneness, give it a ring of O's: *Throw me*

that old snakeball, boy, throw it right on in here,
Thelbert would say, squatted behind home plate,
and the ball said *I have been wrapped in monkeytape*

*long enough, Take this mask off me so I
can gather what dust rolls on my brow:*
the dog on my foot tooths my sock: a fool

dances on my toes, yelling in the bleachers
in the ninth inning: *talk it up, boys, talk
it up: can't hit it when he can't see it:*

*yonder it goes, right in the old tar barrel,
youdababyoudaboy, hustle, cobabe,
coboy*: where are they, the girls with rosy

cheeks and bare feet and lips the color of
cherries hanging over the hedges,
the ground scattered with pits and hulls, what joyful

eating!—the tart juices a surfeit for
the one hit I am waiting to bat, the
chalked circle drawn, and I am marking the

dirt with first my right toe then my left, my
socks just right, my wool cap a perfect fit,
and my turn comes: I step into the batter's

box: the crowd's silent murmur a din of
nothing, a rush of welcome, score tied:
I am there in my stance and the pitch comes

like a pill: I swing and the ball goes out
of the park, over into some zinnias:
I run the bases, and since there is only

one ball I trot out to help find it:
a woman beats me, saying Get your ass
out of my flowers: I feel the bruises

build through my ball suit, the awful humiliation
of intrusion, whereas her sport is definitely
not mine: her zinnias are forever

to her: if you jump a wire fence to get
back into the park to count the runs, total
the tally, when it is all over, all

you can do is lie down, put your hands behind
your head, if you like, sigh, and, if there is
a fly nearby, or dust, a blowing curtain,

the sun coming in through the glass, watch it:
that is yours to keep: so you turn over
in the night, walk the dog that hoists its leg

unconfused, come back and place yourself in
a cool spot, trying to remember that
the bed is supposed to slope, hoping that,

too, was all in your head, a place you come to
among the birches on the long afternoon
walks, the birds and small game animals

announcing in their places, the fox leading
the way: you must not follow me, for worldly
ways are enough: the frog was next, and he said

notice my status between earth and water:
my natural fecundity is not
cunning like the fox, but amphibious

first: you see me when the headlights brighten
the rain falling and we are so many lines
that form from the highway in your vision:

so contingent on not accepting the end,
we bend the period to any punctuation
we can stand: my mind is tended like a plain

grown full of clear places moving in and
out over what's left: the places I touched
as a boy say you are always alone,

but be not afraid: make sure you forgive
yourself often, and keep your means in a thimble:
look at the grass gleaming and know you must

move into a lifting-up exercise:
persist in all motions: do not wonder
if it really matters, for the sky says no,

inspiration rolls over and whimpers:
wait a long time for the world to be on
the least footing, a place to place your

understanding, cornerstone, word, a space
justice fits when you rise to walk out of
yourself to say Here I am, humanity's

boll weevil, family and all, waiting
for you, there, squatted under a pine by
the edge of the marsh, saying to yourself,

or the tree, look at that form, and then it
is gone into luminescences
between your eyes: you turn back toward the creek

to see the beaver's mound and notice the
tail threading through the water, a low
profile in the country I was born to,

stretching to feel the heat in the night's shade,
the best the fallow land can afford for me,
up on nothing except cow manure: naked

as we can be, we repeat the surfaces
of our lives like doodlebugs scurrying
home for the depths, the parting and the entry,

the ultimate emptiness a tingling light
running through the skin: I need more help than
I can give: the wish for harmony, a

lifted arm coming around from adversity,
kicking and laughing my way through a serious crisis,
beauty in the dark, the shadow shod with

blessings of the nimble hour: keep my stillness
adrift, timeless with the river: the moments
flow to the route and rout of circumstance:

*Grandpa was asettin in a chair on
the wagon: the mule slipped in the rut there
right before you git to Rehoboth and*

*the steeple went dangly and your mammy
fell off the board and went down in the ditch
of the hymn your granddaddy was hummin:*

*a Model-T come by and dog if hit
didn't git stuck, too: I got up outen
the mud where I had sot and propped my foot*

*on the running board: I said if this is
the rain's mission, we got a long way to go
to sweet clarity:* a dog lies before

the fire a long time until the folds in
its skin glow with affection: I bear the
insignificant gestures: I have no

adverbs to dangle on my ears or shoestrings:
my friendship beads are my palm and trace,
the thunder and rain outside the stables

where the mules stayed: you learned when the vet came
that the cow *found* the calf, even if you
stood around the corner of the barn and

peeked while Mr. Bill Carroll ran his hand
into the cow and got the calf's head right:
and a mama cat always found kittens:

the same with the sow and pigs: in cold January
I'd go down to feed the hogs and the pink
pigs would be there: the questions received me

like a friend and I remember that world
intact: that hope runs through my misunderstandings:
it parallels the capacity to tour

the modern exhibitions and be grand
in the museums, an humble guide to the universe:
Old Man Wash Bird was a midwife: he was

a bitty little man: he'd get on his
hands and knees and rock directly in front
of the woman in labor and grunt, saying,

"She'll be here any minute, yessiree!"
Where will I go? I need a lease, anything
to hold on to: "Hand me that maul," Uncle

Huel said, "I'll show you how to kill a hog":
he put his feet between two of the boards
on the wall, swung the maul with his right arm

over the side, backed it farther into
a pendulum motion, directing it
toward the hog's forehead, when the weight of the

curve in the swinging maul picked his feet out
of the crack and he pitched over the top
and toppled into the pen: it had been

raining and Huel disappeared in hog
manure: I know where I am going when
I see it coming: I went down to the creek

and saw the tree where the goat's head was hung
and the turtles were there scratching around
the tree, trying to get up to taste the blood:

the tree stayed in the afternoon, livelier
than before: the muffler on the tractor
glows warm and I fall asleep while my brother

makes the rounds, emptying the noise in the
ridged rows of poverty and the forming
stars around the fields we come back to, spreading

a mirage, a corner or a place to
sit in while the world comes to our side like
a battered dog: we wander by the trellis

rotting around the rose in the dooryard
flecked with insects searching for a place to
cling to, as the bees swarm all of a sudden

next to the kitchen window and someone
comes and takes them away over his shoulder
like a hobo's bundle, a chimneysweep,

done, off to doctor soot, shoot the smut from
the chute, free the smoke's root: we lose ourselves
in the creek that reflects our bodies, wavy,

like the funhouse at the fair shooting us
up and down, left and right, distortions, and
we laugh and go our way like the Venerable

Bede's lone sparrow flying in at one door,
and immediately out at another:
like the squirrel bunching on the limb,

mid-stop to nowhere, before it undoes
its white sock of a stomach and then falls
down like a foot, we find the right positions

for our peace and comfort: the hackberries
hang from the limbs, the cool fall days a blessing
after the yellow bus goes away and

you got the day in your arms: you leave the
packhouse and go into the woods to wait
for the leaves to spread a quilt, for the soul's

radiance is large, encompassing grief,
missing the missing word: winter, after
the tobacco had been bundled and sold

and you could turn your palms up to the tin
wood heater glowing in the kitchen, the
eatin-table covered with dress patterns

waiting to be cut: in hog killing time
the sausage stuffer was screwed to a corner
of that table and every turn of the

handle would work out the misery: dust motes
dance in columns on the linoleum rug:
in the kitchen he whittles on sourwood:

thin ice blazes in the hound's water pan
before days stay sunny and warm enough
to walk shirt-sleeved: he whittles holes in sourwood bark:

*When journeys repeat, repeat their interiors
where is the song between winter and spring?*
In the kitchen he plays a flute of sorrel:

one time there were four separate entrances
for moviegoers at the theatre in Red
Springs, North Carolina, one for the whites,

one for the blacks, one for the Indians,
and one for the Smilies who, somebody
said, didn't know who they were: do we know?

across the road is the old Stephenson
cemetery: seventeen slaves are buried
there without markers, anonymous as the dirt:

the hedges fall, the wire fences grow
into the tree trunks: birches break, sun struck,
rain driven, unshelved as junkyards settled

so deep the land reclaims them, pride shaping
a temple where the clutter grows over
the ground, the kudzu, cockleburrs gowning

the red rust: my mother's hand goes like a
bird on a nest, making a crater in
the flour for biscuits, and when she brushed

a lock of amber hair from her face,
she left it white: she was young and beautiful
and now she is beautiful: I put on

a ragged shirt: it was a warm cotton
shirt with the collar half gone: my mother said
I won't ride with you wearing that shirt: we

could have an accident and you could get killed
and people would wonder Who is that man
in that shirt: my thought is to dress for the

highest yield: if I succeed it will be
close: the whole area from Middle Creek to
Cleveland School was called Finch's Mash: I'd look

across the creek to the swamp, floating, lifting
always more at dusk, the shores retreating,
forgetting the whiskey made in the stills:

Henry Finch's gravestone is broken through
the praying hands: "Blessed are the meek for
they shall inherit"—and the rest is gone

like the rattling pods around September
peas we shelled and put up in Mason jars:
we'd drop them into a guanosack

I'd swing over my shoulder and walk across
the road to the barnyard: I'd take a tobacco stick
and thrash the sack and the husks would change to

dust and pulp, rags of hulls, and I'd empty
peas and husks all together in a bucket
and go find the wind to blow the chaff from

the peas: my mother said Winnow the peas:
I am alone in the woods: I thought today
I could bury the feeling with the dying

fleas, but, no: the wind punts the questioning
spirit out of comfort: there is no trick
to settle the fools rushing around my head:

I shall remove my outer matter and
go for the beam: the long run comes around:
across the road from where I was born a

persimmon tree grew, a bleak tree and the
plows always lifted when the mules' heads went
for it, and one day my father said See

that dove sitting on the limb yonder,
across the road in that tree? And he put
the .22 in the crotch of a chinaberry,

got his bead, pulled down on the trigger and
the bird went ragged: I knew the expressiveness
of victory for the hunter there, standing

in the front yard of his shanty, a hero
who would tell his story of killing the
one dove at seventyfive yards: what emblem

the cavemen left on the walls, passing to
us their motifs—the fluttering wings, the
legs lifting and creating a place for

the hunt to carry on: I have no father:
he is gone, a hearse taking him away
on the same road we rode in the '37

Ford pickup: his friends said you will go broke,
but he climbed the hill and started a farm
and helped raise four and now the road leads to

the bottom of a hole: senility
is time's king of spades until the load is
too heavy and can challenge no more but

lift the chunk of dirt from one place and put
it in another, the hole filled and patted
with the shovel a few times, all neat until

our backs are turned and the wind blows the plastic
flowers: before my father died he rolled
his clear blue eyes back and said, "Don't you know

I'm dying?" I was trying to get the straw
in his mouth so he could drink: he told me
I never could pour water in a barrel:

I never could get up a grounder either:
my father would flap the ball and trap it
against the ground: he said he could play second

base with a rag, and he could too: the last
six months were bad: we wanted to feed him
and he kept telling me how he wanted

me to keep his grave clean: he could see us
walking over him, he said (over his
ruined earth and his clothes of the world

rotting away, but never his grin and
the way he held his head high when the gold
flashed in his teeth and you knew the hounds would

run the fox): my father said most people
in this country won't buy anything
unless it costs a lot, saying these people

have about as much sense as the hole right
under a dog's tail: imagine out of that place
my father's grave at Rehoboth Primitive

Baptist cemetery: I can go now and
clean it off, cut the sawbriars and the grass
growing at his feet, read his dates

(1901–1981) and know his days are mine:
prosperity: *Stay here with me
and we'll hunt and fish* fanning the heat

he hobbled away from my breath *I'm going
to college:* alone on my own I left
my guitar at home, the farm boy and his dreams

brought me a style to relive what I
hastened to leave, the white church
the family there in splendor,

a hill clean and breathless: our humanity
is a dimmer to light up hell or poke
through life, bear the cold, the bed making and

the sheet spreading, the questions closer to
riddles than answers: the brood comes around:
the shoes rest under the bed: the sheet does

not comfort: fire cannot cure the nakedness
and the cold: there is no rune we can recite,
not even any hocuspocus for

the amusement of the audience:
I will wake tomorrow: I will have lain
wrong on my neck again: I will be home

with my small means and little bread: it is enough
to sustain the blot, unfoul the morning:
why do I sleep crookedly? Ah, be straight,

body, be deep in peace as the form is
peaceful today: the mire has run: we have
nothing to lose in looking for kindly

faith: it crawls when it cannot walk: grace teaches
us to fear and relieves our senses: there
is a dullness in the bottom of my spine,

a tale of ache and wrack: the twittering
goldfinch says gold until the end begins
to double back as dogs will on a track

to get the fox's scent once more, as fathers
free the fathers in themselves to roam the
streets and streams in old shoes, in the chankings

of the skins of others terrified by Death's
baby grin, the east glistening in the sun:
the ground over our bones may grow better

lovers inside our bodies than any
we can imagine against the ridges
of our lives, our innocence in a basket

full of eggs waiting to break for space, go
for the little and big, do a dance in
every word, the music going round and

out, original and raw, long and short:
Talk about music! I will put the fiddle
on my head and play; bow, backward, bend my

knees, then slide it in the small of my back
and play: my rosin is the color of bourbon:
the varnish on the fiddle is thick

and browned in rolls beyond the tuning pegs
where the neck goes up in a scroll like a
god's imagination: identity

swells and throbs the resonant leaving and
coming together beyond the truth contained
in the turning fall where the body breaks

in the least music, what beautiful agony:
let the darkness come around, one look enough,
the bending like a gypsy's clothes motley

with many charms: gold is in me like an old
nostalgia stumbling to figure the hallowed
mind: Get into the fact: rattle the possibility

of the lost, confused luminescence which
brings the chill, the log and loving head, the
raptured flight of the transfiguring night:

the lover's paradigm comes on the bright
side of zero, a little rendezvous,
untended innocence: what sense of justice

wreathes around home base, the coaches in their
boxes chalked in, absolved, for the way is
ever the winter's tale finishing its

farewell over and over: sway the coming
fall: autumn is the sweetest rush beyond
the too-ripe melons: no time to be sentimental:

we will no longer make breakfast and see
the day through, but court the weeds where our touch
has been: ask nothing of the dirt that settles

in our bones, for we will not shiver again
the slightest dances: the immersion is
close to a song: come and see the lowering

bodies, raised skirts, the feet under the water,
the close contact with a rose that will not
fade: the earth was once enclosed in a sea

of faith; now the darkness is full again:
I surrender it to the upward creeds
in their biding places: the doves fly to

the sunflowers: goldfinches come close to
the hunters for the seed, tributaries
irrational in faith, hope, and space: charity

is inviolate: it is a gorge in
a depth of regard, valid as entering
a room, knowing you are headed for a

chair, the stomach empty as the mind after
a night of trying to sleep on a too-soft
mattress in muggy weather, fleas hopping

up: Winter leaves a tone of mystery
lost in ambient waves of rain, the idea
of instruments: listen to a tin roof sing:

hammers on top, the train whistle: don't know
whichaway I'm riding long as I keep
the balance between left and right, high and

low: the stillpoint is husky, thin, brimming
with pitfalls, loops, lopes, all kinds of surprises:
racecars tracking a wilting lastness, mules,

ears going, slicing the heat waves, the plow handles
down while you wonder how to get through the roots:
you remember the snags in your past:

Roscoe Flowers could snag anything that
came toward third base: he was a short man:
he used a glove with no padding; Barbecue

Hicks was short, too: he would prance at second
and chant, "Hustle, hustle," and he said it
with flair: every jump the squirrel makes from

the shed to the crepe myrtle is different,
just as a window washer's squeegee never
goes the same stroke: the way is to pull the

window down on your stomach and hang out
the air and look up for the moon when every
sound's a rag on glass: the scrap-iron man

would come up or down the hill, stop his truck
to ask Got any iron and we would sell him
an old skillet or plowpoint or Model-T

axle for a nickel: Lord, keep me from
the rags of myself: let me swing a song
the way the people used to walk the road

by our house, dirt roads so muddy with rain
their shoulders sagged: let the pitch strike one more
time, touch the bull's eye sweet center, believe

the space every syllable leaves will flower
truth in the conversations we make at
parties, eyes moving outside our heads,

the fishbowl bubbling filtered water through
algae and scum all the froth after too
much working out in one confinement, suspecting

something to settle deeper on the bottom
as a leadline does when you toss a perfect
cast, and wait: it is no wonder I keep

asking for help: a redbird's beak claps the
feeder and the glass turns into a cymbal,
a flat, heavy ache of slightest hope through

the vines: I need to see myself in one place,
able to stretch in the morning, look out
the back door and notice the grass a duller

green where the dew is dry: why am I here?
Where could I go? Where do I seek refreshment?
I see humility in the diligent

soul: I keep hoping for the ache to break:
I don't know what to do except push my
head and the tips of my fingers until

I move the ceiling, forcing it to speak:
remember the thin covering on everything,
the sound the redbird brings to the window,

the chirp in the hedge: my father took the
Schwinn off the 3/4-ton pickup: Paul
rode it over the yard; the front tire diverted

under the truck-body, the frame up in
the air and the boy's nostrils plowing the dirt:
there was no gang gathered to hoot, only

the way back up from the ground: play the space:
if hummingbirds come, the hot days will be
prayers, players, the sotways will drink to mine

eyes on the rook: perch on the wire above
the azalea, pretty bird: oh the cuckoo
is one who lays clear the sense of being

nowhere: we lean back on elbows, saying
we came from there, the will in the wasp, poke
in the porky twig: when the pitcher hits

the ball, the cow moos her lonely: I want
the crash of the door brought back to reveal
the empty sun casting its pelt on the ground:

the tomb is empty, empty, death's best answer:
blow you winds, cold and old in the pockets:
bring the rain up out of the damp earth's tough stuff:

my rough faith is real: will a ranger know
the field is plain and will the up and down
in it be the same earth, bare, a square cotton

patch of a place with a face, the frown of
October: November remembers the howling
light: a strewn riddle tumbles where the blistered

mountain spreads wings whirring like windmill blades
around the low, humble grain, the futile,
dried fruit of knots and ever: the threat is

dryness: do I care? Those paths October
leaves: oh the narrowness in the clarinet:
I sit in a ditch bank and hunt for my

self among the ragged presences: come
out from the bumpy air: my study is
a haven of heavens when I prop my

feet on the pull-out leaf of my desk and
look out the window, like Woodstock with his
fishing pole, waiting for a nibble to

leaf the hedge and roll my way, say a word
or three about the way to compose a
couplet, for instance: Pope is not a dope:

skip a rope and verse is better off dead
than black and blue: Oh! What a thing is man?
His head like a poppy hangs: his feet hurt:

he works and waits and works: signs of bliss
he's sensed or missed: deep in verse he spent his life:
did Edward Taylor show his Meditations

to his wife? Sprindge, my heart, this is the
moment to sail, my spirit feels hatcheted
today: I have worn the light too long, this

going to and fro, wracked with fortunate
blather and bother, bottles of lotion
left in bathrooms, on tubs, around drains,

mustering a sway beyond the primal
scansion in the line where the drive goes past
the third baseman's glove into left field, an

aria of blood pulsing *I shall not
be moved*: I will keep my old composition
notebooks, roll away paragraphs, the quilt

full and warm in the room: there was no need
for peace: we had it, Lord: keep it for us
now: where there is confusion, grant that it

is in weaving that we are drunk: old men snore
while the catfish bite in the moonshine,
bobbing corks: the drums go muffled and the

dream never is truer than itself: go
out and pick the peas, stake the tomatoes:
the godhead will outlast the groom and the bride,

their stately night, my clear remembered
gardened knot wherein paradise does live
a glorious height: glory surrounds me

on my run, like a dog off-lead, big, little,
short, tall, God, I love them everyone: Slobber
Mouth could outrun the Word of God with the

Bible tied to his tail, this tale told in
the drool of the cow's cud or in a dream
a solitary lover sees when he

nods to the boy in himself going to
the driveins in the little towns, playing
games under the neons: guy-wires tighten

on the streets: concrete breathes: the doorway
wonders if the air will last: when we have
been rented down deep inside our hearts, why

won't the flame move: why, when it may be too
late, do we stand at the gate in the evening,
after the cotton has been lifted on

the weigh-horse, why when the car is in the
road forever headed South does the word
"Romance" come from out of the corridors,

from behind the big hall mirrors, under
the loveseats in dens filled with wall-sized glass?
Rows of mansions protected like a dumb show:

Mencken, R. Baker, Wolfe, Poe, slung shadows
dancing over the projects, a fragile train
carrying Zelda miles from the inner harbor:

what to look for after the old is yellow:
old Baltimore seated at her mirror:
the wisteria around the porch posts

holds the myth still as a suburb across
the tracks, all I may have ever wanted
in my life, a lie true to the next truth

emotions make ready and leave around
the ankles, smoke turning to horizons,
songs, egg houses where graders hum with

country music on the record player
blaring among the fresh smell of cracked eggs,
lots of pretty pompoms shaking up over

the crowds at basketball games so much desire,
the very best tears falling on the homework
of adolescence, arguments slipping down the

night: humming "A Rose and a Baby Ruth"
you sit in the balcony and wait for sweet love
to hold the sweat while the chocolate

in your pocket melts to mounds everywhere
and you wish your pain would just get up and
walk out the door so you can enjoy

"Rebel Without a Cause," but lust sings
in your blood and if you could kindly cut off
your leg for thirty minutes or pick up

the front end of a tractor your clothes
would be themselves as they were in the
beginning, before shade, spring water,

reruns: no myth lingers as a tenant
to save this infirmity of space: what
statues exist as we enter the sanctuary:

you revise what you read once with the right
ending: bear the full measure steeped in the
family's one circle: bring the comedy

to its denouement: fill a space wide as
a Texas waltz, one step out of the hole
filling up with hedges all the experiences

we never see: if we belong to a set
expectation, why do we want to see
it again: it is a sweet dream capable

of the long swoop the Ferris wheel climbs: be
wide as that, go with philosophy you
can manage: if you are not as big as

a country, be a county, or a seat
or a township: just remember to be
all the human you can: raise the ceiling

until your headache craves no more tension,
braves no more saving grace: I'm looking for
the doorjamb to expand so I can call

your name to say I have an answer: it
is uncommon as a shadow in the ruts:
I had no strategies: the yellowed walls

of the packhouse mattered irrelevantly,
the knothole in the barn door shrinking the
green in lonely weather, the blues rolling from

Uncle Henry's lips, his left hand sliding
the Pepsi bottleneck up the strings; behind him
Stephen Foster's darkies rise up out of

the laps of their masters, saying you will
be in our humanity this time: we
will live together as children and grow

old remembering the planked floors baring
cracks, doors open wide, fertile history
waiting for legislatures to set society

spinning with the earth's unspeaking tongues:
there is a pattern of primary elements
running out to the seed taking all my

energy and spreading it among the wiregrass;
so I said to the first green this morning,
if I could find the way to see this feeling

through I could face tomorrow, maybe dance
around the table, loosen my shirt and
relax, and the green came back, lifting enough

space for the jay to swoop through and I got better:
I could see how the sky furnished us again
a motley brush of air for the grey gone

into the foundation of the garage,
the two cars looking like trains, one central,
one sidetrack, as the old painter Thaddeus

said yesterday when he remembered playing
in his yard, some resistance to the pain
joy carries around in a sling so ragged

the words won't come—like some of the undernourished
children I grew up with: I'd see them down
the hill in the clay, digging with spoons: they'd

put it in a washbasin and walk strong
to the tenant house where you could smell the
baked clay as much as a blackberry pie

they'd pick later, in mid July, and the clay
and pie together would be a treat they
never knew better: I'd stand and wait and

Duck would hum a wailing shroud or scarf of
a sound out of the sawbriars on the bank:
I'd wonder and know I could never shake

the experience there, Duck moaning and
saying, Shub, sing me a song and I always
sang about peace, angels, lambs, and black nights

like the sea: oh we were young in our need
for the earth to let us be: we had tenants,
white and black: Marshall Brown, wife Eloise,

daughter Annie Mae; A. Z. James; Lee Terry,
a strong man who could lift a stick of green
tobacco and muscle it straight out, first,

and then stick it up to the hangers on
the tier poles, and his wife Lucy; Elvis Terry,
wife Mae Dinah (whose *feets* were always hurting),

her mother, Molly, who looked like a man
and wore a man's wornout brogans; June Williams
and wife Viola, their children: Roof and

Thelma Allen and A. Z. and his family
were the only whites I remember: Roof
and A. Z. killed themselves: Roof had no father:

A. Z. went broke and drank himself to death:
I knew June best: he carved his initials
in the crown of the chimney of our new house:

I was taking a shower in the basement
when he came down the outside stairs and saw me
and I turned my backside to him and he said,

"Shub, I got one too": Minnie Birch would pick
cotton and she wore a sack dress which fell
in folds over her stomach: she and Duck

and Lil Sis would come to the hill to dig
the clay: and there was Henry Knight and
his wife Mary, their children and grandchildren,

Uncle Henry playing the blues every
which way; sometimes he'd bar the strings with his
pocketknife: I lay down and listened for

the one bird to note what summer brings to
the grosbeak and the old rose-hued finch among
the seeds, the ruby throat in the pink juice—

what glories lay claim to me, the beautiful
changes in my eyes: I was so hungry:
the surrounding hemlocks gave back my feeling

with visions I can name: a rotting bluegill
at the edge of the pond swaying its faint
deadliness, the pale white eyes, marbling, pressing

deeper into the earth growing out of
itself its one song of life, the sounds nature
promises with dogwoods most freely, while

the lambs in the pasture bababa their
charming songs of death from the hillsides,
perception's natural trot away from

irony toward the moment when every rose
lasts longer than its smell and aches no more
than the thorn's pictures we make out of passion

and the dancing cross, the last firstness cut
from the rusting nails in their beams, the chips
rotting in furious pleasures: there must

be an outlet for me in the lay of
the flared seat, the muffler raised above me
like a golden standard, heat waves shimmying

around that stack where wise men and warriors
meet: the sword works at its sorest need: the
foe is bondage and the night: we are ignorant

of what comes before and after, utterly
out of sight from the fair and stormy weather,
and we are not safer here: I strike a light

and mount the stallion: the mare beholds my
distraction: this is the Morgan Family from
down there below Benson, the children of William

and Negelena: Minnie, Aldonia, Geronia, Sophronia, Naomi,
Nebraska, Philaster, P. Jasper, Harold,
Jada, Ruth, Ethel, Perry, Jimmy, Willie,

and Bright: ah, without an ideal, the family
grows and grows: the gentians wave on the
galleries of the drowned lilies: drum,

beat your drum, with a bandage on your thumb:
moan to form a light, because my sweet is
flaunting night: no use to pluck the goose and

lose the feathers to the bed: the shifting
blood flows to the knees: the hard touch draws a
skilled line into experience: toss the apple

from the secret: the myth is music with
a source complete and select: the mockingbird
turns in my head like sculpture handheld and

rubbed away to show the imagination
of that place: I need a mountain to see
me through: my identity is the top

of the rock, my notice the scampering
leaf: I feel the contingent drink of the
green-black bird cracking the fennels: thistles

float, the leaning sunflowers running their
circles to yellow out the eye overhead,
a tally, hoe-helved, crooked surreally:

there goes the sonofabitch, the foxhunter said:
the man in breeches and coat said, "Tally-ho!
kind sir": let go the body: the cardinal

flowers stretch across the landscape, handsome
in their high keys: there goes a plankhouse into
a hedge: we come from a desert of innumerable

dances made in pain and pleasure arriving
forever, America's promise, Huckleberry
laid back every spring when the little green

corn is sided, what broken clods to bounce
in the dirt: the literature of the world
is the people: Whitman, where are you? Our

faculties run out into the unknown:
results are beginning, continuously
extending the plain chance to hold a seat,

here, hardy as a foot soldier: an articulate
voice lowers to let the mind down so the
undergarments might hear humanity

in the bosom stumbling back to breathe independently:
transitory, we bequeath to thee, O Death,
this victorious song thou breaks, the word

of the singer, his parentage and home,
the wood in the flames a quiet crackle
of no hurry going up and out, moving

the dust that settles the ashes, a tune,
a farway injury of happiness,
a bliss that is hard to empty: time and space

affirm the rhythm, the dimensions of
across and around: wrap a tent around
the music and steal away: images edge

the feelings like heels grinding lightly on
a board of closest imaginative
stances delighting the reapers in the

wheat, the keepers in the creek: the word is
another form of dancing: the body
moves on the surface just over truth: we

live amid the skin: the true art of
experience is practiced by the skipper
bugs: they skate so well: I clap my hands and

the water scoots a wake beating with a
new beauty: and the line which begins behind
is brought forward: I look back one more time

to draw a radiance in language, a
radical system formless and grammatically
mountainous and divine, mortal as the

fertilizing rain, a lingering space
that gives the celebration a morning, noon
and night swallowed up by the dallying and playing

world holding the ancient beard in an avenging
dance, a cosmos for jollity: high in
the pocket of a farmhouse I am alone,

a laughing moon brightening like an orange on ice.

SHELBY STEPHENSON lives on the small farm where he was born near Benson, in the Coastal Plain of North Carolina. "Most of my poems come out of that background," he says, "where memory and imagination play on one another." Educated at the University of North Carolina-Chapel Hill, University of Pittsburgh, and the University of Wisconsin-Madison, he is professor emeritus at the University of North Carolina-Pembroke, and served as editor of the international literary journal *Pembroke Magazine* from 1979 until his retirement in 2010. His awards include the Zoe Kincaid Brockman Memorial Award, North Carolina Network Chapbook Prize, Bright Hill Press Chapbook Award, and the Brockman-Campbell Poetry Prize. In addition to *Fiddledeedee*, he has published *Shub's Cooking*, *The Hunger of Freedom*, and a poetic documentary *Plankhouse* (with photographs by Roger Manley), plus ten chapbooks, most recently *Steal Away* (Jacar Press). *Family Matters: Homage to July, the Slave Girl* won the 2008 Bellday Poetry Prize, and the 2009 Oscar Arnold Young Award. The state of North Carolina presented Shelby with the 2001 North Carolina Award in Literature, and in 2014 he was inducted into the North Carolina Literary Hall of Fame.

Cover artist **Hayden Tedder** has been drawing since childhood and began painting seriously in the fall of 2011 when she began studying acrylics with Steven Hopkins. Since then she has been working to improve her skill and style. She is a member of Delurk Gallery in Winston-Salem, North Carolina, and has shown her work in galleries, restaurants, and coffee shops. She has assisted in body painting and curates art shows for the Community Arts Café and other art spaces in Winston-Salem. She says, "I find inspiration in the movement, connection, and communication of humans through nature and technology. I believe that life is lived in the ways we allow it and that anything can be done if we refuse to let excuses block our paths to fulfill our dreams and plans."

www.ingramcontent.com/pod-product-compliance
Lightning Source LLC
LaVergne TN
LVHW041346080426
835512LV00006B/636